Welcome to HMS VICTORY, the flagship of Britain's great Admiral, Lord Nelson, at his finest hour – the Battle of Trafalgar in 1805. She is still in commission in the Royal Navy as the flagship of the Commander-in-Chief Naval Home Command – lovingly preserved as a living testament to those stirring times, and as a source of inspiration to today's Fleet.

We are proud to share with you the world's last remaining Ship-of-the-Line and hope that you will thoroughly enjoy your visit.

The Commanding Officer
HMS VICTORY

In 1758 Horatio Nelson was born, son of a Norfolk parson. In that same year a First Rate Ship-of-the-Line, HMS VICTORY, was ordered to be built at Chatham. Forty-five years were to pass before they finally came together – he as an Admiral of the British Fleet and she as his flagship in the Mediterranean. Their union culminated thirty months later in the Battle of Trafalgar when, on 21 October 1805, in the most decisive battle ever fought at sea, the combined fleets of France and Spain were vanquished without the loss of a single British ship.

During the 18th century Britain's colonial expansion had increased the demands made on the Royal Navy. The naval battles of at least six wars had taken their toll of ships and men.

In 1758 the government decided to build 12 Ships-of-the-Line. Heading the list was

THE FIVE VICTORYS

	Launched	Details
1st	1559	The CHRISTOPHER, a merchantman, purchased for the Navy in 1561 and renamed the VICTORY. Rebuilt 1586. 800 tons; 34 guns; 300 mariners.
2nd	1620	875 tons; 42 guns; 270 men.
3rd	1675	The ROYAL JAMES, renamed the VICTORY in 1691. 1,486 tons; 100 guns; 754 men.
4th	1737	1,920 tons; 110 guns; 900 men. Built at Portsmouth. Lost in the Channel with all hands, 1744.
5th	1765	The present HMS VICTORY now in No. 2 Dock at Portsmouth. 2,162 tons; 104 guns; 850 men. Built at Chatham.

LAUNCHED AT CHATHAM DOCKYARD 7TH. MAY 1765.

EXTREME LENGTH 226'-6".   LENGTH OF KEEL 151'-3"
EXTREME BEAM 52'-6".   DEPTH OF HOLD 21'-6".
LENGTH OF GUN DECK 186'.   TONNAGE 2,162 TONS. DISPLACEMENT TONNAGE 3500TONS.

ARMAMENT.

LOWER DECK 30 LONG 32 PDR. MIDDLE DECK 30 LONG 24 PDR. MAIN DECK 32 LONG 12 PDR. UPPER DECK 12 SHORT 12 PDR.

a First Rate of 100 guns, the largest ever ordered for the Navy. This decision created the same interest, and had a similar effect on the public purse, as would the ordering of an aircraft carrier today; by the time of her launching in 1765 she had cost £63,176. The keel of the ship that was to become 'Nelson's VICTORY' was laid down on 23 July 1759 in a drydock at the Royal Dockyard, Chatham.

There was at first some doubt about whether this new ship should be called VICTORY, since the previous ship of this name had foundered with all hands. But 1758 turned out to be a year of victories for Britain, and the doubts were overcome. These same victories eased the pressure on the ship-building programme and VICTORY was not fitted out for commission immediately. She remained in her drydock, and, by the time she was launched on 7 May 1765, her great oak timbers were fully seasoned – a crucial factor in her subsequent preservation.

The 38 years which followed before the destinies of Nelson and the VICTORY united were times of almost continuous war and tension for Britain. The fall of the monarchy in France, the French Revolu-

tion, the War of American Independence and the rise of Napoleon kept Europe in uproar and England under constant threat. By 1803, Nelson was a national hero many times over, rising through storms and battles to be a Vice Admiral of the White and a Viscount. He had scandalised society with his amatory adventures but had retained the nation's trust. The VICTORY, also by now a battle-hardened veteran, was to be his flagship after her refit at Chatham.

ARMADA	1588	SOLE BAY	1672
DOVER	1652	SCHOONEVELD	1673
PORTLAND	1653	TEXEL	1673
GABBARD	1653	BARFLEUR	1692
SCHEVENING	1653	USHANT	1781
FOUR DAYS BATTLE	1666	ST. VINCENT	1797
ORFORDNESS	1666	TRAFALGAR	1805

ABOVE: *Battle honours board. The present* HMS VICTORY *saw action in the last three engagements.*

LEFT: *Entry port on the port side to the Middle Gundeck.*

MIND YOUR HEAD

FAR LEFT: HMS VICTORY's *details displayed on the Lower Gundeck.*

A t this order the drums rolled for 'Beat to Quarters', and the men hooked up the hinged bulkheads
- stowed the officers' furniture in the hold
- removed the stern windows
- prepared stern chaser gun positions
- cleared the lower decks
- secured sails, rigged chain preventers on the yards and hung safety nets (to catch falling men or broken spars)
- poured water over the sails, boom, boats and hammock rolls (to reduce the fire risk)
- set up the ship's fire engine on the poop
- filled fire buckets, laid hoses and sprinkled wet sand over the decks (to prevent men slipping in blood later)
- swayed boats out for towing astern (they would be needed after the action)
- prepared the guns.

Preparing and firing the guns was a skilful and highly disciplined operation. Each 32-pounder needed a crew of twelve men plus a powder boy, or monkey, to

LEFT: *Powder barrels stowed in the Grand Magazine, from which individual charges were made up.*

BELOW: *The Lower Gundeck, housing thirty long 32-pounders, where the crews lived between their guns.*

TOP RIGHT: *The carronades. Invented in 1779 at Carron, in Scotland, these short, light ($1\frac{1}{2}$ tons) guns, firing very heavy shot (68lb) at close range, wrought havoc at Trafalgar.*

BOTTOM RIGHT: *The Middle Gundeck housed 28 of these 24-pounders. Carpenters, sailmakers and cooks worked on this deck.*

operate it. The powder monkey provided the flannel bag of gun powder (prepared in advance and stored in the hanging magazines) needed each time a gun was fired. The bag was rammed down the muzzle into the breech, followed by a wad, the round shot, and then another wad. All were rammed in hard. Meanwhile, the Gun Captain pierced the flannel bag with a pricker down the vent, and inserted a quill containing powder and wire to provide continuity from flintlock to cartridge. He then put loose powder into the flintlock pan and the gun was 'run out' by its tackles. The Gun Captain cocked the flintlock, pulled on the firing lanyard, and the gun fired. The action of firing caused the gun to recoil to some three feet inside the ship, where the breech rope took the strain, and the rest of the tackle held the gun firm whilst the crew cleaned it. A reamer on a stave was pushed down the muzzle and quickly withdrawn to remove any smouldering fragments of charge. A wet sponge on a stave followed, to clean and cool the barrel. Then the business of loading began again. This whole loading/firing cycle could be carried out in 90 seconds by a well-trained crew.

It is a measure of the Royal Navy's effective discipline and morale that the seamen they employed, about half of whom were pressed men and 'quota men' (miscreants who had elected to serve their sentences in the Navy rather than the horrors of an English prison), were trained so well that they could clear a ship like VICTORY for action in less than ten minutes. Napoleon's Admiral Villeneuve, so thoroughly defeated by the Royal Navy under Nelson at Trafalgar, remarked after the battle,

"The act that astonished me most was when the action was over . . . the English immediately set to work to shorten sail . . . with as much regularity and order as if their ships had not been fighting a dreadful battle. We were all amazement, wondering what the English seamen could be made of. All our seamen were either drunk or disabled, and we, the officers, could not get any work out of them. We never witnessed any such clever manoeuvres before, and I shall never forget them."

After the French Revolution, continental Europe fell under the domination of Napoleon and his Grand Army. However, Napoleon never fully understood the strategic importance of sea power, nor did he give his Admirals the full support they needed to defeat 'those far distant, storm-beaten ships, upon which the Grand Army never looked, but which stood between it and the domination of the world'.

By 1803, Britain and France were again at war and, when Nelson embarked in the VICTORY on 18 May, his simple mission was the total destruction of the enemy's fleet. The French Admiral Villeneuve did his best to avoid direct confrontation with the British fleet and he attempted to draw his adversary across the Atlantic, leaving the English Channel exposed to French control long enough for Napoleon to invade England. But Nelson's superb

ABOVE: *The Battle of Trafalgar (so called because Cape Trafalgar was the nearest point of land) at 12 noon.*

BELOW: *'Trafalgar at 2.30p.m.' by W.L. Wyllie R.A. VICTORY breaks free from the REDOUBTABLE.*

RIGHT: *Nelson's Prayer before the Battle.*

seamanship and tactical brilliance enabled the British to outsail the French ships in an epic chase. Subsequent foul winds and false reports of the British fleet drove Villeneuve to Cadiz. He knew that Napoleon was sending another Admiral to relieve him and he determined to sally forth with his combined fleet of French and Spanish ships for the fatal encounter that he had for so long avoided. The stage was set for the Battle of Trafalgar.

Early in the morning of 21 October 1805, the French and Spanish ships were sighted and at 7 a.m. the VICTORY hoisted the signal 'Prepare for Battle'. Nelson retired to his cabin for a few minutes and his Flag Lieutenant, Pasco, following him

ABOVE: VICTORY's *guns in position. It is estimated that, at the Battle of Trafalgar, the French and Spanish crews took at least twice as long as the British to fire their guns, thus giving the British double the fire power.*

down with a report, found him on his knees writing the prayer that has become part of England's heritage.

When the VICTORY had closed to about 1½ miles from the enemy, Nelson said, "I'll now amuse the Fleet with a signal – Mr. Pasco I wish to say to the Fleet 'Nelson confides that every man will do his duty'." Lieutenant Pasco, after consulting Popham's code, said, "If your Lordship will permit me to substitute 'England Expects' the signal will be sooner completed, since the words are in the vocabulary and the others must be spelt." Nelson replied, "That will do, Pasco, make it directly."

At 12.40 p.m., with a tremendous explosion, the VICTORY fired her first broadside at Villeneuve's flagship, the BUCENTAURE. Her port carronades, loaded with musket balls, raked the BUCENTAURE's decks, smashing her stern, dismounting twenty guns, and killing two hundred men.

"May the great God, whom I worship, grant to my Country and for the benefit of Europe in general, a great and glorious Victory: and may no misconduct, in any one, tarnish it: and may humanity after victory be the predominant feature in the British Fleet.

For myself individually, I commit my life to Him who made me and may His blessing light upon my endeavours for serving my Country faithfully.

To Him I resign myself and the just cause which is entrusted to me to defend.

AMEN • AMEN • AMEN"

In one terrible broadside the French ship was effectively removed from the action. A moment later, the VICTORY ran aboard the REDOUBTABLE and broke the line. Behind her the TEMERAIRE, NEPTUNE, LEVIATHAN, CONQUEROR, BRITANNIA, AJAX and AGAMMEMNON followed in quick succession. Twenty minutes later Nelson was struck down, shot by a musketeer in REDOUBTABLE's mizzentop 50 feet above him. As he was carried down to Surgeon Beatty in the cockpit, he placed a handkerchief over his face and orders so that the ship's company would not recognise him and be disheartened.

Down in the darkness of the cockpit, cut off from the action, Nelson had been stripped of his clothes and covered in a sheet. He was under no illusions about his fate. "I am a dead man, Hardy. I am going fast; it will all be over with me soon. Pray let my dear Lady Hamilton have my hair and other things belonging to me." A little

LEFT: *This plaque, with its simple inscription, marks the spot on the Quarter Deck where Nelson fell, mortally wounded, at about 1.25p.m. The actual planking on which Nelson fell has been relaid in the Cockpit where he died.*

RIGHT: *'Close of Day' by W.L. Wyllie R.A. The frigate* EURYALUS *prepares to take the* VICTORY *in tow.*

BELOW LEFT: *'Death of Nelson', by A.W. Devis, who came on board at Portsmouth when the ship returned from Trafalgar, and sketched from life all the people gathered round Nelson.*

The "Remark Book" of Mr. R. F. Roberts, a Midshipman in the VICTORY.

"The hull is much damaged by shot in a number of different places … Several beams, knees and riders, shot through and broke; the starboard cathead shot away; the rails and timbers of the head and stern cut by shot; several of the ports damaged and port timbers cut off; the channels and chain plate damaged by shot and the falling of the mizzen mast; the principal part of the bulkheads, half ports and port sashes thrown overboard in clearing ship for action. The mizzen mast shot away about nine feet above the deck; the mainmast shot through and sprung; the main yard gone; main top mast and cap shot in different places and reefed; the main topsail yard shot away; the foremast shot through in a number of different places and is at present supported by a top mast, and a part of the topsail and crossjack yards; the fore yard shot away, the bowsprit jibboom and cap shot, and the sprit sail and spritsail topsail yards, and flying jibboom gone … The ship makes in bad weather 12 inches an hour."

later on, Hardy came below again and congratulated Nelson on his victory, telling him that fourteen or fifteen of the enemy had surrendered. "That is well," whispered Nelson, "but I had bargained on twenty."

Nelson's Trafalgar tactics had worked well. He had driven his two columns through the enemy at right angles, dividing them into three groups. Thus divided, they had been compelled to fight three separate battles, deprived of mutual support.

Every one of the thirty-three British ships returned from the battle, but of the forty enemy vessels, nineteen were taken as prizes, of which only four were saved.

Trafalgar broke France as a maritime power and freed England from the threat of invasion. Subsequent British naval supremacy enabled Wellington to campaign with secure lines of supply by sea in Spain and Portugal and on to the decisive battlefield at Waterloo in 1815. This supremacy was not to be seriously challenged again for a century.

Particulars

Length on Gun Deck	186' 0"
Length of Keel	151' 3"
Moulded Breadth	50' 6"
Extreme Breadth	51' 10"
Depth in Hold	21' 6"
Displacement (approx.)	3500 tons
Burthen	2162 tons

Maximum speed in fair weather
with all sails set was about 8 knots

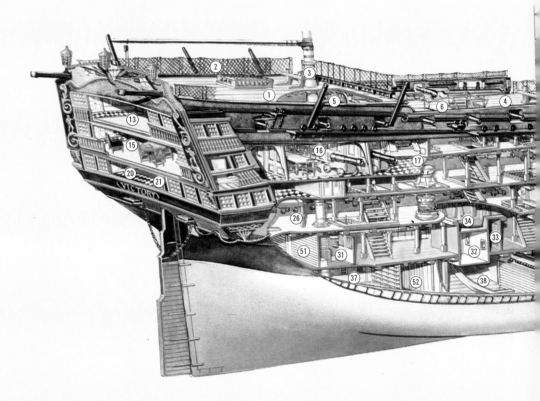

1. Poop Deck
2. Hammock Nettings
3. Mizzenmast
4. Quarter Deck
5. Ships Wheel
6. Here Nelson fell
7. Pikes
8. Mainmast
9. Belfry
10. Fo'c'sle
11. Carronades
12. Foremast
13. Captain Hardy's Cabin

14. Upper Gun Deck
15. Nelson's Day Cabin
16. Nelson's Dining Cabin
17. Nelson's Sleeping Cabin with cot
18. Bowsprit
19. Middle Gun Deck
20. Wardroom
21. Tiller Head
22. Entry Port
23. Capstan
24. Galley and Stove
25. Lower Gun Deck
26. Gun Room

Armament – 1805

Lower Deck	30	32-pounders
Middle Deck	28	24-pounders
Upper Deck	30	12-pounders
Quarter Deck	12	12-pounders
Forecastle	2	68-pounders (Carronades)
	2	12-pounders (Bow-chasers)

At extreme range (about 1 mile), the shot from
a 32-pounder gun would penetrate 2 feet of oak

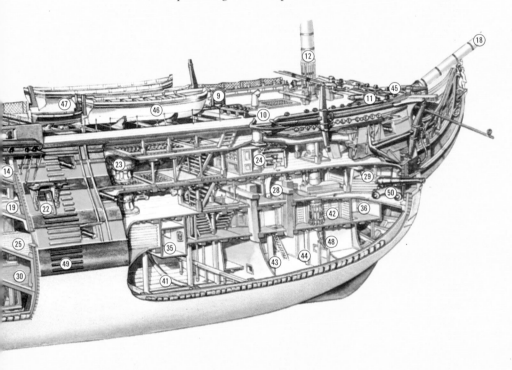

27. Elm Tree Pump	40. Bilge Pumps
28. Mooring Bits	41. Main Hold
29. Manger	42. Gunners Store
30. Orlop	43. Main Magazine
31. Dispensary	44. Filling Room
32. Aft Hanging Magazine	45. Marines Walk
33. Lamp Room	46. Admirals Barge
34. Midshipman's Berth – here Nelson died	47. Ships Launch
35. Forward Hanging Magazine	48. Light Room
36. Powder Store	49. Boarding Steps
37. Powder Room	50. 32lb Cannon
38. Aft Hold	51. Bread Room
39. Shot Locker	52. Spirit Room

In the bows, on the line of the lower gun deck, are four hawse holes, two of these being used for 24in. hawsers which run to the two bower anchors used for mooring the ship. When weighed, the bower anchors were hauled up to the catheads, which project from either side of the bows and which were furnished with sheaves or pulleys. Catheads were always gaily decorated, generally with a lion or a cat, but in the VICTORY the decoration is in the form of a crown. The two empty hawse holes were used for hawsers of the two sheet anchors, now lashed outboard on both sides of the upper deck.

When the ship was anchored, the hawsers were secured to the riding bitts which are securely bedded down in the ship's structure. These 24in. hawsers were too large to be taken by the main capstan on the lower gundeck, and they were operated by an endless 15-inch rope known as a messenger, secured to the hawser by short flexible lengths of rope as the hawser entered through the hawse holes, and which were untied before the hawser pas-

LEFT: *The original figurehead was much more ornate than the present one, which dates from the long refit of 1801–03, when the ship was brought forward for service as Lord Nelson's flagship.*
RIGHT: *The anchor in the foreground is that by which the* VICTORY *was moored when lying in Portsmouth harbour from 1812 to 1922.*
BELOW: *The Main Capstan (on the Lower Gundeck) is repeated on the deck above on the same spindle, so that 260 men could weigh the anchor. The ornamental top of the centre-line capstan could be removed and space was then available for the ship's fiddler, who played a merry tune as the men heaved at the capstan bars.*

The ultimate development of the wooden sailing man-of-war, the VICTORY, is 227 feet long and 52 feet in the beam. She mounts 104 guns of various calibres and, fully manned, carried 850 men. In Nelson's time, ships were painted to suit the taste of individual Captains and Admirals, and the VICTORY is painted to suit Nelson's personal choice, called by the Fleet 'Nelson's Chequerboards'.

VICTORY rests in dock today on specially built cradles so that her normal water line level is parallel with the top of the dock. This makes it possible for the visitor, standing by the bows, to look down into the dock and see her beautiful lines, which were used as a pattern for many years after her launching.

The keel, which now rests on keel blocks, is made of elm and oak. It is 152ft 3in. long and of 20in. square section, with a false keel of elm 4in. thick. The hull itself is made of English oak, with outer and inner skins, and is over 2ft thick. Below the water-line, the ship was coppered with 3,923 pieces, each 4ft by 1ft. The coppering was added in 1780 as a protection against the teredo worm.

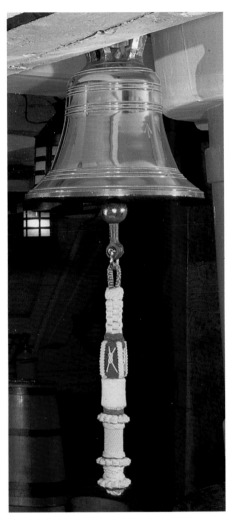

sed through the deck to the cable tier below. This process was known as nipping. The short ties were secured by the powder monkeys, who were known as nippers. The messenger rope passed round the capstan four times, was eased in its passage by stout rollers on each side of the deck, and the particular direction of movement of the 260 men on the capstan bars weighed the port or starboard anchors respectively. The iron pawls at the base of the capstan could check its movement if necessary.

For other hoists 140 men could be put to work on the centre-line capstan (on the Middle Gundeck).

The three masts – fore, main and mizzen – tower above the deck and rise respec-

tively 182, 205 and 162ft from the level of the dockside and waterline.

HMS VICTORY has 27 miles of standing and running rigging and under all plain sail she set 4 acres of canvas. She would have had three complete suits of sails, plus additionals such as stuns'ls, royals and stays'ls for calm weather and light airs.

HMS VICTORY now normally wears the Union Jack at the jackstaff, the White Ensign at the stern and at the main topgallant masthead, the flag of the Commander-in-Chief, Naval Home Command.

The stern post emerges from the lower gun deck, and secured to it is the rudder, the movement of which is controlled by the tiller, which is operated by ropes leading to the steering wheel.

ABOVE LEFT: VICTORY's bell on the Middle Gundeck. The original was shot away as she closed the enemy at Trafalgar.

ABOVE: View forward from the Poop.

LEFT: The Poop Deck seen from the Quarter Deck. From this deck the famous signal "England Expects ..." was hoisted. The binnacle contains two compasses of the Trafalgar period. The steering wheel was operated by 4 men in calm weather, 8 men in rough.

Life in a great sailing battleship like the VICTORY was hard for every man on board, be he Admiral or powder boy. No one was exempt from the cold and wet, the ship's motion, the lack of privacy, the rancid food, the fetid water, and from months at sea without touch with the land. It is not surprising that the most common ailment in the Navy was rheumatism, and it was no respecter of rank. These factors apart, however, the life styles of officers and men were very different.

Nelson's quarters occupy the middle rank of windows in the stern. He had a dining and day cabin, and a sleeping cabin. In the day cabin Nelson discussed with his officers his plans for forthcoming battles. Today, a picture of Lady Hamilton still adorns the dining cabin, and the day cabin contains a table and an armchair which were in daily use by Nelson. His body lay in the day cabin after his death before being disembarked at Sheerness in December 1805, prior to his burial in St. Paul's on 9 January 1806.

The sleeping cabin contains the folding bedstead used by Lord Nelson, a combined wash and toilet cabinet and a cot, both typical of those used by Sea Officers of the period.

The Admiral's and officers' cabins were all parts of the respective gundecks. Consequently, when preparing for action, all the cabin furniture and the partitions would be wrapped in canvas and stowed away either in the holds or in the boats which would be towed astern.

Most of the crew lived on the lower

RIGHT: *The Great Cabin, in which Nelson shared meals with his officers. The colour scheme is a faithful replica of that existing at Trafalgar. All the chairs fold for storage. The table breaks down into twenty-two pieces.*

BELOW: *Nelson's cot, the drapings of which are replicas of those made for him by Lady Hamilton, which are now in the National Maritime Museum. These replicas were made by HM Queen Mary at the time of the original refurbishment.*

gundeck. At sea it would have been as dank and dark as a dungeon. With the gunports lashed closed, a dim light filtered down from the gratings above, and everyone lived by the light of candles and lanterns. They ate at the mess table, between the guns, and slept in hammocks slung from the deckbeams in two tiers, 14 inches of width to a man. They received two cold and one hot meal a day; fuel for the galley fire was precious, and the fire was only lit once a day. The water, stored for months in casks, was described in a contemporary account as "the colour of the bark of pear trees, with plenty of maggots and weevils

in it". The same account describes the ship's biscuits as "Making your throat cold in eating it, owing to the maggots which are very cold when you eat them, like calves foot jelly, or blancmange".

The men lived for their daily rum ration, the great pleasure of the day. In those days it was $\frac{1}{2}$ pint a day per man. For the junior ratings it was mixed with two parts of water and issued half at midday and half in the evening. This mixture had to be drunk at once, or it went flat, and thus prevented men from hoarding their rations for a drinking spree.

At the after end of the main gundeck,

screen doors opened on to a different world. This was the wardroom where the commissioned officers lived. Dominated by the great stern window, painted white, and furnished with 18th-century elegance, it provided a stark contrast to the squalor of the gundecks.

The orlop deck, below the gundeck, housed the junior officers, including the surgeon. In battle, this dank and airless place became the operating theatre and hospital, where, by the light of guttering candles, hideous splinter wounds were tended and amputations performed without anaesthetic.

ABOVE: *When a man was punished by flogging he had to make his own 'cat-o'-nine-tails'. After use it was flung overboard and salt rubbed into the wounds, to reduce the risk of infection. Captains could not order more than a dozen lashes without a court martial.*

RIGHT: *The Surgeon's Cabin on the Orlop Deck, with a portrait of Surgeon Beatty who attended Nelson at his death. Both it and the Dispensary were near to the Cockpit which was used in action as a surgery. The red colour scheme disguised the presence of blood.*

LEFT: *The rum ration was an essential pleasure to look forward to twice a day. It was called 'grog' after Admiral Vernon, who started the practice and who was called 'Old Grog' after his grosgrain boatcloak. The 'tot' was by no means always rum – it could be brandy, wine or beer, depending on availability. When it was beer, often substituted in British harbours, it was a massive 2 gallons a day per man.*

TOP RIGHT: *Hammocks were slung between guns on the lower gundecks. Each man made his own hammock and was allowed 14″ of hanging space. 550 men lived on the Lower Gundeck.*

BOTTOM RIGHT: *When not in use hammocks were rolled, lashed and stowed in the nettings on the Upper Deck. The mess tables were shared by 12 sailors plus one boy, who had to clean out the spittoons (most sailors chewed their tobacco as smoking was allowed only in the galley).*

Portsmouth Naval Heritage Area
Information for Visitors

HMS VICTORY

HMS VICTORY is open every day of the year (except Christmas Day) from 10.00 am to 5.30 pm (last tickets sold at 4.30 pm). Exact opening and closing times vary between summer and winter and precise information can be obtained by telephoning Flagship Portsmouth on 023 9287 0999 (www.flagship.org.uk) or Portsmouth Tourist Information Centre on 023 9282 6722 (www.visitportsmouth.co.uk)

Shop

Good quality souvenirs of HMS VICTORY and the Royal Naval Museum are available from the HMS VICTORY/Royal Naval Museum Shop.

HMS WARRIOR

The towering masts and distinctive 418-feet hull of HMS WARRIOR now greet visitors to the Portsmouth Naval Heritage area. When she was built in 1860 she marked a revolution in warship design; in her day she was the world's largest, fastest, best protected, most formidable warship, with her iron hull and armour plating.

She has now been restored to her original condition.

MARY ROSE

King Henry VIII's famous warship, the MARY ROSE, was raised from the Solent sea bed in 1982, where she had lain since she sank in 1545, fully manned and equipped for battle.

Her hull can now be seen in a specially converted drydock adjacent to HMS VICTORY and there is a separate exhibition featuring a wide selection of the objects recovered from the ship.

You've seen the ships: now meet the men!

Alongside HMS VICTORY stands the Royal Naval Museum, the only one in Britain devoted to the overall history of the Royal Navy. Here, the ghosts of past seamen are brought vividly to life in a series of exciting, modern displays that tell the story of our Senior Service from earliest times right up to the present day.

Exhibits include figureheads, ship models, uniforms, medals, relics of personnel and ships, paintings and prints and commemorative silverware and pottery. Pride of place is given to the possessions of ordinary officers and seamen and the displays concentrate on the social history of the Royal Navy.

There is an extensive library and a documentary and photographic archive which are available to researchers by appointment.